Backyard Friends "Sing-A-Long"

Author & Illustrator:

A good man protects the life of the animals:

Proverbs 12:10

To order additional copies of this book, contact:
Xlibris
844-714-8691
www.Xlibris.com
Orders@Xlibris.com

ISBN: 978-1-4363-4093-9 (sc)
ISBN: 978-1-4363-4094-6 (hc)
ISBN: 979-8-3694-0125-5 (e)

Library of Congress Control Number: 2008904094

Print information available on the last page

Rev. date: 10/03/2023

One little squirrel sitting in a tree.
One little squirrel sitting in a tree.
One little squirrel sitting in a tree.
Hey, he's looking at me!

The Squirrel eats berries, nuts, corn, insects, & seeds. They raise 2 to 5 babies way up in a tree.

One hummingbird eating something sweet.
One hummingbird eating something sweet.
One hummingbird eating something sweet.
Hey, she's looking at me!

The Hummingbird eats insects sometime and nectar from flowers by the hour. They lay 2 eggs the size of black-eyed peas and make their nest with spider webs and leaves.

One red bird singing in the tree.
One red bird singing in the tree.
One red bird singing in the tree.
Hey, he's looking at me!

The Red Birds (Cardinals) eat fruits and seeds and make their nests low in little trees. They raise several young throughout the year so we hope the red bird will be here for years.

One blue jay eating bird seed.
One blue jay eating bird seed.
One blue jay eating bird seed.
Hey, she's looking at me!

The Blue Jay eats insects, fruits, nuts, & seeds and makes its nest high in a tree. They make their nest with twigs & dry leaves and lay greenish/blue spotted eggs with 3 to 5 little babies.

One woodpecker pecking on a tree.
One woodpecker pecking on a tree.
One woodpecker pecking on a tree.
Hey, he's looking at me!

The Woodpecker eats vegetables, nuts, insects, & berries. It lays 3 to 10 eggs in a hole of a dead tree where it likes to raise its family.

The Red-headed Woodpecker is endangered because we are cutting down dead trees where it likes to raise its babies.

One little wren feeding babies.
One little wren feeding babies.
One little wren feeding babies.
Hey, they're looking at me!

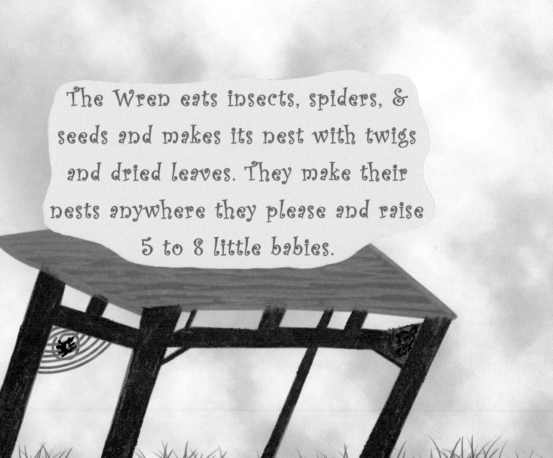

The Wren eats insects, spiders, & seeds and makes its nest with twigs and dried leaves. They make their nests anywhere they please and raise 5 to 8 little babies.

One chickadee flying around the tree.
One chickadee flying around the tree.
One chickadee flying around the tree.
Hey, he's looking at me!

The Chickadee eats insects, seeds, & berries and makes its nest in holes in a tree. They lay 5 to 8 tiny spotted eggs and live in deserted woodpecker's nests.

The Doves eat grains & seeds and make their nests in bushes or trees. They lay 2 white eggs with babies inside and take care of them both day & night.

The Dove was used in the story of Noah's Ark. To read more about the story go to Genesis chapter 8 in the Bible.

One mocking bird singing melodies.
One mocking bird singing melodies.
One mocking bird singing melodies.
Hey, he's looking at me!

The Mockingbird eats fruit, insects, earthworms, & bees and it doesn't like anyone in its territory. It makes its nest low in little trees then lays 3 to 5 eggs that are blue-green.

The Rabbit likes to come out at night to eat and play in the moonlight. They have lots of babies throughout the year & love them oh so very dear.

All of the animals looking at me.
All of the animals looking at me.
All of the animals looking at me,
to keep them
SAFE & FREE!

Saving our animals, one animal at a time!

Saving our planet, one tree at a time!

"Sing-A-Long" Song

About the Author

Kimberly grew up on a farm where she raised over 75 rabbits, walked baby goats on leashes and bottle-fed baby cows. She also hatched baby geese that thought she was their mom and followed her everywhere. She is now a stay at home mom who homeschools and is always looking for fun and entertaining ways to educate her own children. She has used music to teach her special needs child how to read and write. She has also used the wonders of raising Labrador puppies to teach her children the responsibility of providing good homes for each puppy. Kimberly and her family love wildlife and want to help endangered species through education and awareness of what it takes for species to survive.

Printed in the United States
by Baker & Taylor Publisher Services